THE ILLEGAL AGE

ALSO BY ELLEN HINSEY

*Mastering the Past: Contemporary Central and
Eastern Europe and the Rise of Illiberalism* (essays)
(Telos Press, 2017)

Update on the Descent
(UK edition: Bloodaxe Books, 2009
US edition: University of Notre Dame Press, 2009)

The White Fire of Time
(US edition: Wesleyan University Press, 2002
UK edition: Bloodaxe Books, 2003)

Cities of Memory
Yale University Series Award
(Yale University Press, 1996)

Magnetic North: Conversations with Tomas Venclova
(US edition: University of Rochester Press, 2017
UK edition: Boydell & Brewer, 2018)

The Junction: Selected Poems of Tomas Venclova
Edited and translated by Ellen Hinsey
with Constantine Rusanov and Diana Senechal
(Bloodaxe Books, 2008)

*The Secret Piano: From Mao's Labour Camps to
Bach's Goldberg Variations* by Zhu Xiao-Mei
Translated by Ellen Hinsey
(AmazonCrossing, 2012)

ELLEN HINSEY
THE ILLEGAL AGE

2018

Published by Arc Publications
Nanholme Mill, Shaw Wood Road
Todmorden, OL14 6DA, UK
www.arcpublications.co.uk

Printed in the UK by TJ International, Padstow, Cornwall

978 1911469 37 7 (pbk)
978 1911469 38 4 (hbk)
978 1911469 39 1 (ebk)

Cover image © Paolo Pellegrin / Magnum Photos
KOSOVO. Town of Pec. 2000.

ACKNOWLEDGEMENTS
Grateful acknowledgment is made to the following periodicals, books
and anthologies in which selections of this work have previously
appeared or are forthcoming: *The Irish Times,* "The Illegal Age"
(Reprise); *Der Tagesspiegel,* "Das Zeitalter der Rechtswidrigkeit", ("The
Illegal Age") German translation by Margitt Lehbert; *Conjunctions,*
"Internal Report / From the Principles of the New Logic", "Internal
Report / On the Rise of the Inconceivable"; *The Southwest Review,* "The
Final Era of Brightness"; *The Missouri Review,* "Terminology Lesson";
The Cortland Review, "On the Progress of History"; *The Wolf Magazine,*
"The Annals of Evidence"; *The Warwick Review,* "The Illegal Age"
(Prologue); *Spiritus,* "The Four Horsemen"; *The Long White Thread of
Words: Poems for John Berger,* "The Laws".
    "Carved into Bark" was presented at a special evening in English
and German translation at the Hamburger Bahnhof Museum in Berlin,
September 2015.
    For support during the time this book was written, the author
would like to thank Katharina Narbutovic and the DAAD Berliner
Künstlerprogram.

Editor for Arc's International Poets series
James Byrne

*The first essential step on the road to total domination
is to kill the juridical person in man.*
HANNAH ARENDT

*My Time, my brute, who will be able / To look you in the eyes
And glue together with his blood / The backbone of two centuries?*
OSIP MANDELSTAM

Forgive me for what I'm telling you.
OSIP MANDELSTAM

CONTENTS

PART ONE

INVESTIGATION FILE
SMOKE

PART TWO

INVESTIGATION FILE
ICE

PART THREE

INVESTIGATION FILE

OBSCURITY

PART ONE

INVESTIGATION FILE

SMOKE

I.

THE ILLEGAL AGE

(Prologue)

I.

Nothing happens quickly: each day weighs on the next –
　　　　Until the instant comes – *nothing happens quickly* –

It takes time for a figure, who makes his slow way along
　　　　The foggy lane in innocence, to vanish – for tables

II.

Laid with silver – for the simple woollen hat twisted
　　　　In rough hands when prayers are said. It takes time

To not suffer the pain of others – to not hope for just
　　　　Mercy. *Nothing happens quickly* – the ravaged book

Of the ancestors remains open – rustles – *persists* –

III.

So when did it happen: was it in the mired trenches
        Of winter – when gas laid waste to limbs hidden

In the reaped, tunnelled mud: but even then, the lessons
        Were not conclusively learned – the pale young men

Not fully alerted: still carried, close to the breast, letters
        From home and pocket bibles; had not yet understood

IV.

The impending facts. *Even on that first September morning* –
        There still remained certain dregs, residue, artefacts –

The Polish cavalry setting out – in full uniform – to meet
        Panzers in a wet autumn forest – among the poplars:

So can we say it was then, the precise instant of change,
        Or was it before – or, in the near, approaching *after* –

V.

Though for some time yet, plans were still drafted in ink,
        And in a rare second, a hand might hesitate – fear,

Like a covenant, tentatively restraining a winter sleeve –
        Even if one was *under orders* – so, when then did

It happen: at what late hour – what longitude – where
        Along the map's axis in Poland's captive heartland –

VI.

Situated on what lost, unnamed path in Ukraine –
        When was it that decency stumbled, at the slick edge

Of a muddy wayside, interred under a simple mound
        Of stones – marked with the hasty, lashed crossroads

Of wooden staves – *nothing happens quickly*, still
        There are indications, signposts, turns along the way –

For we must know exactly where it was lost, to erect
        There a monument: to the advent of the *Illegal Age*.

(i)
"The starry sky above the thinking reed
and the moral law within it..."

II.

Evidence

THE LAWS

ARTICLE 1.

It is forthwith declared: if by the land of their ancestors
they are *strangers* – so shall their children be *strangers* too –

ARTICLE 2.

If so identified as *strangers* – they shall no longer be fit
to dwell under the common, rough-timbered sky –

ARTICLE 3.

If they labour in the cities, they shall no longer reside
in the cities; if they live in the country, they shall be
deprived of even the wind-scattered sheaves –

ARTICLE 4.

If thus, they find themselves without labour: *their
idleness shall be punishable;*

ARTICLE 5.

And, if the Laws have once pronounced judgment upon
them: they shall be forbidden speech in the crowded
market square –

ARTICLE 6.

If they find themselves without land, wealth or voice: the *stranger* shall live within the tight confines of the journey –

ARTICLE 7.

Where hours shall be their daily bread and rustic nightfall their only shelter –

ARTICLE 8.

And if, by chance or destiny, a *stranger* should love a *non-stranger*, they too shall be punished –

ARTICLE 9.

Nor shall they benefit from counsel in the white interrogation rooms.

ARTICLE 10.

Where iron hooks shall be roughly affixed to pillars in Justice's basement.

ARTICLE 11.

And although those in attendance shall bear false witness, they will be exempt from forty stripes –

ARTICLE 12.

For no one shall preside over the Laws: *for my beloved, have no doubt – we too are the generation of the Flood.*

(ii)
*"Have 'they' been to our house… or are
'they' there even now?"*

III.

File 53291

ELEMENTARY LESSON
IN DIVISION

[Exhibit A]

Start, as once instructed, on the left side of
the equation: there you will glimpse the totality
of a simple, well-ordered room – lamp on heavy
table, sideboard for bread – zero and numeral of
cup and utensil; beyond will be the parenthesis
of plain carved kitchen chairs, the absolute
volume of milk, the infinitesimal decimals of
poppy seed and rye – add to this the hallway's
length with boots aligned, the small bedroom
with skull and torso washed, and the oak bed
with its justice of sleep –

From the sum of this scene, now deduct the
darkened parlour, the kitchen in low light, the
stairwell with its moon-pierced pane; subtract
again until you arrive at the integers of a forced-
open suitcase, woollen jacket, undershirt, comb,
fragile photograph, and folded psalm –

Then, reduce this further – distil it into collapsed night, pare it down to the pure number of wagon car and silence – divide again until you arrive at that single digit where all universes converge, all is reduced to one, where only a fraction of the face is left visible, then only a mouth, only a black eye through the bars – before the prison train jolts.

CONFIDENTIAL DOCUMENT I

IV.

INTERNAL REPORT: ON THE RISE
OF THE INCONCEIVABLE

[1.]
Genesis
The Inconceivable first emerges along the periphery –
discreetly agitating on the edges of local chaos.

Reception
At the outset, it is supported by few – *even opposed by
many*. Unconcerned, it doesn't suffer its anonymity.

Beginnings
The Inconceivable lashes out with the impetuousness
of an inexperienced, tense blade. Provocative, it traffics
in the outskirts of meaning.

Advance
Biding its time, the Inconceivable seeps forward
mastering territory with the unpredictable sleight of a
storm's stealth –

Reach
Until what stood at the periphery attains the centre:
until the Inconceivable gains access to *the human heart*.

Ownership

Privileged Position

The Inconceivable's ascendency allows it to proclaim:
few own the earth equally.

Postulate Regarding Expertise

Ownership of the earth is an advanced science, rarely
understood by the common mind.

Erudition

Fortunately, the Inconceivable has fully mastered the
Laws of Selection.

Popular Refrain

*With honour and pride I will reclaim this earth, my homeland,
from my enemies –*

Inside Information

The Inconceivable alone knows that The Tribe is a form
of *perfection.*

Cartographic Mystery

Why, in time, the flawless contour of the Perfect Tribe
fails to touch the familiar curve of the earth.

[3.]
Methodology

Aplomb

To enforce the Laws of Selection, the Inconceivable is aware a high degree of sophistication is in order.

Method of Human Engineering

Above all, a strict methodological hierarchy must be observed.

Pyramid of Loss

To avoid, at the outset, any inconvenient objections, the Inconceivable knows to begin with the lower castes.

Proven Theory

One poor person, more or less, will not trouble the sleep of the burghers.

At First

Disappearances are carried out like the sudden vanishing of a ragged-winged bird over the far horizon.

Auditory Particularity

Remember: the empty silence left behind the *disappeared* is unlike any other.

[4.]
Practicum

Further Expertise
To forge The Perfect Tribe, the Inconceivable knows it must undertake a campaign against the *untidy nature of being.*

Review
To so do, the Inconceivable renews its acquaintance with technology.

Range of Options
The Inconceivable never underestimates the usefulness of the humble, as well as the sophisticated, weapon.

Full Sweep
The Inconceivable soon refines its ability to adjust disorderly limbs and temper unruly gestures – all neatly gathered into its Ultimate Order.

Unfortunate Detail for The Inconceivable
A prison is often near a road; a forest by a village; a ravine close to a farm.

A Form of Reassurance
The Inconceivable knows that before dawn, at least for a time, the streets can always be washed clean of blood.

[5.]
Stature

Upstanding Character
Overall, The Inconceivable believes itself of clear mind and conscience, and as such, a model of ethical comportment.

Pure Intentions
The Inconceivable merely hopes to serve The Tribe, which has graciously placed Absolute Power in its hands.

Materialism
Even truth's stubborn clay can benefit from its prowess – ingeniously moulded into a superiorly satisfying form.

Fortuitous Coincidence
If, along the way, the Inconceivable reclaims ancestral homelands, gathers lost faithful or expands the territory of tidiness – who would oppose it?

Dictum
Rare is the individual who can attempt the complexity of existence without the guidance of a Protector.

Footnote
Little matter that even Brutus's descendants were already, years ago, slain.

[6.]
Bellum Contra Populum

Inevitability
In time, the Inconceivable tires of the thicket of its own rhetoric, eventually revealing its true motives like a stiff wind exposes a cliff face.

Bureaucratic Cannibalism
The Inconceivable knows it is only a matter of time before its own Tribe members will be submitted to the Purges of Perfection.

Enduring Conceit
Few are those who can conclusively remain above suspicion.

Disquieting Caveat
But even this, the Inconceivable holds, is not a cause for sorrow.

Truism
One can never say that the Inconceivable ever lacked the ability to think big.

Totaler Krieg
For the Inconceivable, *existence* itself becomes its ultimate target and goal: it's always been a sort of final solution.

(iii)
"Now when I build, I shall begin with smoke from the chimney…"

V.

Evidence

HANDBOOK OF SMOKE

1.

MATERIALS

You can construct it on frozen earth; erect it from split wood and strung wire.

2.

LATITUDE

You can decree a location next to a forest; beyond the close hearing of a town.

3.

GEOMETRY

You can implant rustic barracks in rows, shackle them in a tight grid.

4.

CONSTRUCTION

You can erect in each corner a tower's spider; dig the harsh terrain for simple latrines.

5.

ENVIRONMENT

You do not need nature's forgiveness; you only need its mute complicity.

6.

PROCEDURE

You can receive the rust burdened trains; you can assemble the thirst afflicted bodies.

7.

RADICAL WILL

You can then do what will never be able to be described in language.

8.

FINIS MUNDI

From each mouth you can erase the sacred vowel lodged at the base of speech.

9.

REVERSAL

In black retreat, you can then tear down the smoke consumed towers; you can empty the silence oppressed barracks.

10.

OBSCURITY

You can disperse the torn identity papers; you can hastily sow the fields with young poplars.

11.

FOREWARNING

Despite how clean the end is, see how much can still be traced.

(iv)
"Oaken door, who hove you off your hinge?"

VI.

VERBATIM

Ukraine, 1942

[Exhibit B]

There is no other way to describe it.

As if the world's sight had been torn away. As if an angular bird, paralysed on a roof's edge, sensed acts beyond the realm of the tongue. Tracked ruin in the wind's ashen logbook.

But, in the end, nothing can be foreseen –

The dirt-splattered trucks unloaded the men. They had their instructions – but the instructions had no discernible border; no threshold.

Instead, they took them where they stood –

In the doorway, by the oaken fence. Where water was quickly drawn, or where bread was interred in the oven. Or in the barn's obscurity, where captive also, the animals had no release from their turmoil –

So forced up against clapboard

Together they fell – bodies laying slain against flanks in the warm milk of new blood. And the sky above them became a crater, and below them the land recoiled, shuddering three times, before settling back like a basalt slab into mud;

Behind the wooden house

Where blunt, scored logs were stacked, the bodies were piled. On the wet ground, rain-filled weeds delivered their grief. Far off a dog, unchained to day, barked, went mad. Rats burrowed into the uncompromising earth. There was a black trumpet-blast of silence –

A trumpet of staggered air

But there were no words afterwards. So none were said.

(v)
"How can we unlearn the silences that inhabit the mouths of the dead?"

VII.

Testimony

THE FOUR HORSEMEN

Warsaw, 1944

When, on that Final day, the heavens' thunderous
black trumpets announced a siege of absolute darkness
– only to roar crimson with a temper of hailstones –

And there followed a terrifying silence, as if the hoar-
frosted epoch of after the stars had begun – which, for
so long, had seemed eternally nailed to the sky;

And the globe's noble sphere was derailed in its
practiced eclipse;

When the good, rich, beneficent earth – mainspring of
all enduring sustenance and staff – was engulfed in an
avalanche of cinders;

While bodies, creeping up through ruin staggered
forth, heaving for breath, seeking oxygen already torn
from the mystery of the atmosphere;

Only to be drowned in convoluted plumes of ash-
clotted smoke –

And from darkness's depths, all were awoken to the treble of the vengeful birds of prey, descending through the slaughter of that eternal night;

While the dead lay in the streets; their bodies not properly lain in the tombs;

When, on that Final day, all the words ever created, all syllables sprung from the gnarled lexicon of Jesse's human tree, these too were consumed in the white, fiery blasts –

For, as had been foretold – the meek dragged forth in their rags, the poor lamented for bread, the fortitude of the strong did not give recourse, the wisdom of the just went unheeded –

When all these things came to pass, as they once did, as they do now –

And still the four horsemen do not come.

PART TWO

INVESTIGATION FILE

ICE

VIII.

Report

THE FINAL ERA OF BRIGHTNESS

I.

You could sense it approaching, over the close border:
        It did not have a specific homeland, it did not hold

A single passport. But it had been long in the making –
        This odd brightness, this new dawn – drawn from

II.

The untiring motion of sturdy gears – so well known
        Along the stalwart boulevards of the modern city –

For day had become *powerful* and *useful* as it blasted
        Through the old – *no*, it had been gathering speed

As it crossed the unmarked expanse of the new century –

III.

And it had company, drew strength from the visionary,
From the labours of the pragmatic; now it was just

A matter of logic – an inherent problem of graphs:
So that, hereafter, *all might be properly appraised* –

Employing shrewd application of sober principles –
That would prepare the way to the *final brightening* –

IV.

For if *mass*'s sovereign density could be penetrated,
Naturally *men* might be squared into the unerring

Accounts: so when it arrived, the *brightness*, it wasn't
New, but untested: hadn't yet accumulated the data,

The unassailable evidence of experience: if doubts
Persisted – if initial application demanded force –

V.

Still, surely, it hadn't foreseen the sun-drenched fields
Of flowing grain – whose sparse allotments left

The outcast to drown in black famine – hadn't imagined
Bodies' lamenting presence by the granite prison

Blocks, hadn't envisioned iron trains disappearing into
The dark – with only small, carved scraps of bark

VI.

Flung from windows as evidence of the disappeared –
            It couldn't have anticipated this, that *bright beginning* –

With its mounting assurance and megaphones ringing
            Out the news of the conquering of the ultimate space

Of the human soul. Still, there are those who saw it –
            Saw that hidden deep in its sure, immaculate grip –

Was the ancient sin of immodesty.

(vi)
"Before the night extinguishes it…"

IX.

Evidence

CARVED INTO BARK

Kolyma, 1952

First Lesson

Remember: each memory salvaged from tyranny's flood is an unsteady, but miracle-buoyed raft.

Second Lesson

In exile's transit, fill your palm with living water; crowd your eyes with the tension of hawk-wing and the holy constellations.

Third Lesson

If you cannot fully remember, then you must invent: until pure invention recalls the forbidden truths.

Fourth Lesson

Sew fragments of psalms near to your breast; later you will understand they represent your only worldly goods.

Fifth Lesson

Virtue too can be muddied like a fist; but even in imperfection, it brings a scrap of forgiveness to the table.

Sixth Lesson

Resolutely cast your lot with the innocence of birch-white; pledge your loyalty to the thistle's fugitive blood.

Seventh Lesson

When abandoned to the thicket of their impenetrable rhetoric, loosen behind you scraps of logic to point the way back.

Eighth Lesson

And though they will use everything at their disposal, remain steadfast: bear up tenacious as ivory – unwilling as leather.

Ninth Lesson

It is said a photograph's torn edge beneath the tongue allows the dead to speak.

Tenth Lesson

In the motion of the eternal planets, divine a map leading out beyond the century's disasters.

Eleventh Lesson

For, even a single word carved into bark is an instant saved – for the unforeseen hour when the Great Trumpet sounds.

(vii)
"Your legs rattle like blue ice..."

X.

File 72194

THE NORTH

[Exhibit C]

Battered tin and the smell of smoke and urine. Morning not even a faint rumour behind trees when the butchering wind stumbles across the threshold. One by one, always with fever— one by one with kidneys aching, shuffling out towards the forest's abyss –

There, the frozen hours unfold, an incessant river; time welded together by the thinnest smelt of memory. Only scavenged fragments to remind that the past once existed: images that return later in dreams with their scenes of love or regret, which upon waking – and turning towards the lice-infested wall – force out a tear, for their immodest tenderness –

Maybe the end will come unexpectedly, a sudden reprieve: but more likely the body will be felled by the axe of the heart, buried in the nowhere land of exile.

No, more likely the end will never come – so absolute is the Master's empire: with its sovereign wilderness of canals, forests and steppes. Still, perhaps one miraculous day: a letter – and the unimaginable will bring you to a street address, a familiar door, real and touchable – but advancing tentatively, your limbs will suddenly rattle with fear: your hair now ashy, your manliness extinguished, your voice rust-encrusted –

Until that time, there is only work, the single mystery of the world. Your thoughts remain encrypted in salt. At nightfall: the trial of bread, the weary tin of soup.

And the conviction that the end of the world is near.

CONFIDENTIAL DOCUMENT II

XI.

INTERNAL REPORT: ON THE INTIMATE DAYBOOK OF POWER

[1.]
Origins
Power's origins are always humble. The small provincial farm, the modest lodge near the remote mountain pass.

Myth
Power likes to evoke these beginnings, to remember its youth among the simply-dwelling.

Agrarian
Humility for Power is like the modest sheen of wheat that rises in beneficent summer light.

In the Meantime
Power minds its manners, listening to others, wiping the boots of its predecessors.

Long-term Strategy
In Power's cob-webbed barn, its innocent sheen plots explosion.

[2.]
Glorious Task

The Decree
Power decides to galvanize the Good Will of the people
for its Glorious Task.

Common Working Premise
Even people unworthy of Power can be made to
contribute to its Glory.

Disquieting Discovery
A body's raw timber can be used – as easily as wood –
to stem a rip tide.

Tragic Accounting Velocity
The speed with which human bodies can be added
and subtracted from the sum column.

Grotesque Coupling
The monstrosity of thought married to an indifferent pen.

Mathematical Problem
How many bodies does it take to build a century?

Brave New World
God remains silent, lest the generations rise from the
dead.

[3.]
Theory

Cherished Supposition

Any failure of Power's Glory is to be found in the hearts and minds of those who hold beliefs foreign to Power.

Standard Addendum

So universally loved is Power, dissent can never arise from native soil.

Indisputable Conclusion

This explains why Power's failure is always a matter of treason.

Exponential Quandary

The ever-increasing number of traitors is a secret matter of perplexity for Power's statisticians.

Medical Theory

It has long been known that treason is highly contagious: easily transmitted by alphabet and glance.

Prayer

Let there be light, that it might shine in the darkness of theory.

[4.]
Criminal Code

Review
To fully comprehend the true importance of Power's Glory,
a complete course of education is always advised.

Preliminary Lesson
Hunger is the first, and most efficient, tool of instruction.

Alternative Method
The truncheon is also a master of discernment; it can
easily identify suspect kidneys.

Insight
Even a solitary cell, quiet as a monk's retreat, turns the
mind to higher reflections.

Elementary Precept
The true path is always accessible to the willing.

Expediency
Of the thousand ways to leave a cement chamber, Power
knows the most efficient route is in a wooden box.

[5.]
Love

Intimate Reflections
At night in private, Power stares forlornly in the mirror, secretly heartbroken that it isn't better loved.

Nostalgia
Power keeps a neat clipping file of its triumphs.

Thoroughly Cliché, but Not Outmoded Strategy
Power hopes that the People will eventually come to love it, or if not, cease to exist.

Nostalgia II
Power likes to drive the same car as its predecessors, so it can feel like a grown-up.

Mythology
Even Power would like to imagine that the spectre of red it sees, just over the horizon, is the beneficent dawn of a new day.

Power's Blindsight
Power doesn't like to be reminded that it watches over day through a bloodied monocle.

[6.]
The Turn

Prospects
In time, Power devours itself like climbing ivy
exhausting a decayed trunk's girth.

Disquieting Allegory
Fragile are the thin, strangled ribs of the subdued and
disappeared.

Beginnings
Power laments for the days of its youth, when it seemed
the sun had shown simply on innocent fields.

Transalpine
Nevertheless, Power persists in having its bust carried
to the top of every snowy alpine peak.

Mythological Virility
Power looks pathetic in old age, hunting wild animals
and sunken tesserae, affirming a show of masculine
force.

Power's Secret Fear
What began as a lie, remains a lie; burrows deep.

(viii)
"The prison always remains at the centre…"

XII.

Evidence

THE PROCEEDINGS

1.

We will now proceed to the interrogation of the accused –
– *Despite the blackly triumphant, the eternal reign of Force –*

2.

Face the judges: begin by clearly stating your name –
– *Because of language: eclipsed and ransomed in a*
stony vault –

3.

Be precise: make your remarks succinct and to the point –
– *Because, under the ancient, remorseful heavens, not*
all that is executed can be pardoned –

4.

Answer the questions that have been put before you –
– *For even if Force has razed the fertile pastures – even*
if its maddened chariots—

5.

Remember you have limited time to give your testimony –
– *For even if only a stoic fragment, a tense syllable*
remains at large –

6.

Any attempt to intentionally circumvent the proceedings –
– To affirm that, in the ultimate hour, fear alone will
not master the kingdom –

7.

Never forget that you are at the mercy of the court –
– That conscience, steadfast, can remain upright on
its fragile, but resplendent Throne –

8.

There is evidence that it was your sworn intention to –
– For those dispossessed of speech – those condemned to
what grieved deep –

9.

We have reliable information that there are still others –
– That when all is finished – all decrees enacted with
the supremacy of iron, there still remains –

10.

Your concluding statement will now be entered into the record –
– The building of Justice's ephemeral, but majestic, kingdom
in air.

(ix)
"Green, yes, hung, yes, under spiteful skies…"

XIII.

File 53291

THE DENUNCIATION

East Germany, 1979

[Exhibit D]

Now she understood: all was blackly clear. The apartment was fixed with accommodating plaster, consensual sockets and acquiescing glass – but, in the end, there was no need for wires. How much better: he was right by your side, in the unassuming afternoon, in the encroaching evening: his breath at your shoulder even in the rough-hewn waking hour –

Now, as you rewind the film, each unguarded moment stands suspect, exposed: was it under summer's watchful sunlight, when together you sat by the braille of a restless lake – or after, returning along the road – was it *then*, when he kissed you *there* – by the prying, iridescent eye of the butterfly – *or was it after*, when entwined you listened to the circuitous advance of night winds –

Was it *then, then, then,* or even, in the impossible *after* – when he had instilled children in you in the absolute moment of conception, viewed only by the perfect mind of God: was it almost immediately, or the morning after, or had he waited, in decency, a few days, a few hours –

You imagine what followed, picture it there in the locked metal drawer: all the captured syllables, phrases – a carbon mine of syntax glittering like black ore in a brown cardboard folder –

Your mind's film stops. Runs forward – back. You focus on his face. *Stop*. Again. *Back*.

Would it be a lie to say you suspected? There have been enough lies. Still, you reload the image, asking yourself now, with all the moments exposed: *didn't you once sense it?* In an inexplicable hesitation of his jaw, in his eye's dulled glint – *in his mouth's suddenly, bitter, spittle?*

(x)
"The black and white era which does not want to end…"

XIV.

Testimony

MOSCOW DEBRIEFING

Together, alone in the discrete hours of afternoon – by the ancient route of executions – you had instructed:

Remember to forestall judgment: beneath the exhausted slag-stone, in the capital's unassuming centre –

You can still hear the unconsoled, rustling voices of the dead.

Hanging directly above it, a plaque – like an imperial bas-relief in tinctured bronze – quietly celebrates the axe and the gag.

Notice how the unreliable light, not yet cleansed of its deeds, lies sinister nearby on the sidewalk.

It acknowledges it too has been an accomplice: it failed to speak out and administer mercy.

And, don't be fooled – simple utterance is still the first to be hunted down and held hostage: roughed up and forced to sign certified confessions.

From a rifled drawer, you brought forth a map – *in a rust-clad warehouse on the city's abandoned outskirts, resistance has been kidnapped across national borders, thrashes in the black net of a new century.*

The eternal prison is still in operation.

You hastily continued: *draw close enough to scrutinize the indecision in their eyes – after the terrible epoch, few are innocent.*

In the distance, as of old, there is nothing but a Bell, an Open Field and the Eternal Lie –

And for us, the Bell, far-off, is soundless.

Like those who will come after, we will now inhabit the windy, disinherited house of the present.

Leaning in, you said hoarsely: *never forget, to live differently is still a form of treason* – there will be those who are hung for it.

PART THREE

INVESTIGATION FILE

OBSCURITY

XV.

Report

THE ANNALS OF EVIDENCE

I.

If there were orders, we were never informed, rather –
        We'll learn of their swift fulfilment only when

After the low raids of night – a light remains along
        The distance's far expanse: *if there were orders* –

II.

We'll know of them simply by veiled, stray words –
        Conveying the unstateable in language that cannot

Be grasped, nor fully denied: *"This morning, bodies*
        Amassing at borders," there, stunned by hunger,

Will be those abandoned to destiny's arbitrary will –

III.

In those unwritten hours – we will awake, listen –
    Reticent to signs, but anticipating the final count –

Though the facts will drift, abruptly shift to conceal
    Purpose, bend to match the now ever-expanding

Range of excuse and permissibility – while we are
    Left to decipher the contours of iron aftermath –

IV.

Experience, again, the unhinged absence of order –
    The city centre – undone / the houses – scourged

By fire / a single staircase – spiralling to the height
    Of no heaven – these last traces of intentionality

Meant to obscure. Yet we are tied to their dross –
    Inheritors of the bare script of their directives:

V.

The campaign / ended at dawn / strategic targets /
    / The bombings were based on reliably gathered /

Site obscured / unmarked equipment / the front /
    / The hospitals had been evacuated / train quays /

We denounce any civilian casualties / be swift /
    / The operation / the troops bore no identification –

VI.

All prisoners' rights – / tentatively, you place
    An unmarked document on the desk, survey

Scarred photographs, filmy diagrams, graphs:
    Watch as rain beats against opaque windows –

Observe mute transcripts growing, a living cell:
    If there were orders, we were never informed –

Yet the task remains: someone must order the evidence.

(xi)
"Word, be that part of us, enlightened,
clear and beautiful…"

XVI.

Evidence

TERMINOLOGY LESSON

1.

EXTRAORDINARY RENDITION

When I was led out, the distance between home and exile lengthened like a frayed rope under the eternal scourge of stars –

2.

SECRET DETENTION

In this place, where I possess only blind sleeplessness and the dust of hours in my mouth –

3.

STRESS POSITIONS

And my body, in its eternal limitations, is twisted beyond the tight boundaries of the flesh –

4.

STRESS POSITIONS II

For where can this flesh go – beyond those fixed boundaries –?

5.

SPECIAL TECHNIQUES

And if this finite body be broken –

MILD, NON-INJURIOUS PHYSICAL CONTACT

I will still possess only these legs and feet – only my
palm's dry imprint; the grey shale of my eye's iris –

7.

SLEEP MANAGEMENT

Lord, do you still watch over me as I sleep?

8.

SPECIAL QUESTIONING

Like each creature, beneath my tongue I possess a Word,
given at birth – a Word that means to be *and* to praise *–*

9.

FEAR UP

And when before thee Lord, we were afraid, and before
your justice –

10.

SEXUAL HUMILIATION

And in the Garden, when we were suddenly made aware
of our nakedness, we hid from God –

11.

BLACK SITES

Where then is this place that I find myself, filled as it is
with the stony absence of Knowledge?

(xii)
"For night unfolds the map, keeps secret
its aim…"

XVII.

File 81724

ELEGY FOR THOUGHT

[Exhibit E]

It's late. Night's cast-off debris rises, rattles the windows. A car below, belligerent, roars, writing the final sentence of the day. The dross of events piles up. Beside the rumpled sheets, the radio, speaking its own dialect, repeats its litany of fears. In the mercury-obscurity it seems the window's transparence becomes the last frontier between here and there. Few questions are asked. And then fewer. It is as if thought itself had been replaced.

A vacancy for its house posted.

Go to bed. It's late. Now only myth is needed. Thus, before night's sleep, visions unfold like scenes from antiquity, blurry beneath the bedside lamp. As of old, the tyrant quickly rises up from a sea of words, and around him men, emboldened, bend low and light their torches. In the dark, the radio's words drip and bend, end where shadows reach the wall's base, then fall to the floor. The unproven runs in rivulets under the shadowy door.

Go to bed. It's late. That's what the radio says: turn out the light, until finally all you can glimpse is your own reflection in the dusky bedroom mirror. No matter what's happening out there, in here you're safe. Listen to the hum of voices that come, overlap, and undo sense into its separate parts. Logic's outmoded and it is only in dreams that a voice will recall

We cannot replace thought with anything.

CONFIDENTIAL DOCUMENT III

XVIII.

INTERNAL REPORT: ON THE PRINCIPLES OF THE NEW LOGIC

New A Priori

The hinges of logic are malleable; manmade. Only simple tools are necessary to pry them apart.

A Common Type of Proof

The mere fact of logic's vulnerability proves the arbitrariness of its nature.

Further Theorems of the New Logic

Conclusively establishing a coherent "sequence of events" is now suspected to be a cryptic form of oppression.

Postulate under Consideration

Relinquishing the ability to determine a "sequence of events" is viewed to be a sign of greater sophistication of intellect.

Question of Consequence

Who is establishing the precepts of the New Logic and exactly what they intend.

[2.]
The Facts

Prior Truism
The Facts – previously accustomed to their modest identities – merely hoped to serve, like willing, steadfast relatives.

Late Discovery
It is now known that The Facts are suspiciously unreliable: their loyalties can never be entirely counted upon.

Unexpected Event
To their astonishment, The Facts have found themselves on the no-fly list.

Further Transmutation
The Facts, alarmed by their sudden notoriety, don't understand why they are sighted in hostile crosshairs.

Peculiar Development of Consequence
After reflection, The Facts have taken shelter in a survivalist bunker.

Banal Cliché Turned Strategy
The Facts must never be allowed to get the upper hand.

[3.]
The Argument

Significant Addendum
Those who are availed of The Facts – like The Facts themselves – are by association suspect.

Dangerous Corollary
To develop an Argument is to take matters into one's own hands.

Analogous Fate
Upon leaving its house, the Argument too finds itself hustled into a black van, duct tape plastered to its mouth.

Devolution
Without The Facts, the Argument risks becoming an extremist, trafficking in recycled words gleaned from handbills blowing down the vacant street.

Red Flag
Discernment is the most dangerous enemy of the New Logic.

Surreptitious Warning
Remember to approach the Argument discreetly: lest your presence be detected and noted.

[4.]
State of Emergency

Fortuitous Collaborations
The New Logic, a genius of innovation, has decided to join forces with the New Laws.

Obsolescence
The Old Laws, ponderously rigid, are now understood to be obstinately burdened by symbol and ceremony.

A Type of Freedom
Indeed how liberating it is – to be done with the gavel, the stone pillars – and the stoic marble *fasces lictoriae.*

Modernization
The New Laws require less cumbersome oversight and welcome a flexibility of means.

Archeological Site
Hidden in the depth of the ancient desert are the two stone judges: *one without hands, the other erect with upcast eyes.*

A Pilgrimage of Sorts
The New Logic, as we speak, is approaching the ancient grotto – armed with explosives.

[5.]
Press Releases

Review and Notification
Please be advised: you are no longer encouraged to grasp the greater operation.

Forewarning
Don't be surprised if, above your head, the white drone of aircraft blots out the words.

Aide-Memoire
Remember: your loyalty is to the technicians of the New Logic, and not to logic itself.

La Vita Nuova
Rest assured: this time there will be no resplendent vision of paradise – no heaven of beneficent salvation.

Only Available Option
To praise the virtues of the private life: beside the bedside lamp quietly cultivate a private relationship with the Facts.

New Logic's Future
Essential theorem to be learned by heart: "From this time forth our mutual annihilation is entirely without significance."

(xiii)
"The unspeakable (…) steals over the land…"

XIX.

Evidence

THE ILLEGAL AGE

(Reprise)

You too have felt it: the imperceptible shift in latitude.

The way the air resistedly parts before the iron wedge of storm.

Later, you will recall you once sensed it – in the instant of darkness before daybreak, for which we have no name.

Do not think it has not been prepared; do not think there are not those who are waiting.

Later, you will remember the air smelled of precision; you will recollect how doubt wordlessly descended.

Was it in those final moments, when they were led down to the water before the terrible act, that you first suspected?

You too will believe you were alone to perceive the tenebrous advance heralded by manacles.

A way forward has been made for the hour without mercy.

Later, you will recall how each letter tightened in the throat; the tongue stammering into silence.

Don't think your compliance is not being observed.

Later, you will realize that compromise is the wood that burns most brightly in the hour before regret.

But by then, all the doors will have been marked in yellow chalk.

Still, let us not pass each other this final time, without recognition, without looking each other in the eye.

Remember: in the ink-light of testimony, a record may still be kept.

(xiv)
"Tell me, love, what I cannot explain…"

XX.

File 94329

JUSTICE

[Exhibit F]

"She recounted how – at dawn's first hour – they went down to his house: the one who had, before the revolution, been guilty of dark crimes against his people. He lived on a narrow road, in a common house, pressed tightly among other houses. They went to his door, and under the sky's mute tribunal, dragged him downstairs into the street. There, they stripped him naked and, before those whose lives he had sewn with fear, they beat him senseless until his body gave way before their restless justice. Blows unto death, and then – even after death – until they were sure he had been carried to where God's final judgment rests.

"But unfinished with revenge, they strung him roughly up by his feet. Like Hector's body, they ceaselessly dragged him behind in the street, circling the city as Achilles once did the ancient walls of Troy. Yet his body, mortal, was unprotected by grace, and bore the punishment of their blows, while a gun arrowed blunt insults into his flesh. Yet later, after deep night fell, in the hour of justice's wake, she turned towards her love in the suddenly unfamiliar dark and asked:

'Tell me please, for I have forgotten, did we too once touch each other with these hands?'"

(xv)
"Our godhead, history, has reserved us a grave..."

XXI.

Testimony

ON THE PROGRESS OF HISTORY

History, it can never be said, was short on ideas.

Each day there were rustic barges to float down green waterways; young timber to fell in distant forests.

There were the Empires to build: borders to survey over where coal-winged birds nested in hedges far from the fires of the native hearth.

There were languages to create: History stirring up a compound of linguistic tincture – touched by the yellow vowels of the *Hellenes* and the dark-thatched consonants of *Germania*.

In all this, History was egalitarian. None were spared the iniquities of fate.

Capitals by the sea were sown with salt – while the genius of deserts prospered: Carthage's soil was white ash when, beneath the star-embroidered sky, Arabic scholars divined the heavens and conquered holy algebra.

History was rarely winded. History was always up-to-date.

Possessed of such prowess, History was naturally ambitious: though crimson blood crazed the paving stones of squares, and horses were driven mad across *champs de guerre* – history dreamed of stability:

The spectre of the *Pax Romana*, its head high, bearing its standard down through the centuries.

Yes, History was confident, unconcerned by detail: even as fingers, like birch twigs, were torn from hands; even as the Good were awoken at dawn and brought to trial.

Truth's green branch twisted in History's dark knoll.

But History's heroics, it seems, are unappreciated: History's luggage has been found full of regrets, last seen abandoned in a ditch.

History, it has been reported, is tired.

NOTES

INVESTIGATION ONE / SMOKE

(i) *"...The starry sky above the thinking reed and the moral law within it..."* Wisława Szymborska, *View with a Grain of Sand* (London: Faber and Faber, 1993), 78.

(ii) *"...Have 'they' been to our house... or are 'they' there even now?..."* from Klemperer, *Diaries*, 1942 (London: Weidenfeld & Nicolson, 1998), 122.

(iii) *"...Now when I build, I shall begin with the smoke from the chimney..."* Leopold Staff, in Czeslaw Milosz, *Postwar Polish Poetry* (Berkeley: University of California Press, 1985), 2.

(iv) *"...Oaken door, who hove you off your hinge..."* from *Selected Poems of Paul Celan* (New York: Norton, 2001), 21.

(v) *"...How can we unlearn the silences that inhabit the mouths of the dead?..."* from personal notebooks 2003-2015.

"The Four Horsemen"
This poem depicts, in part, the 1944 razing of Warsaw after the Uprising, "In the Market Square of the Old Town, unexploded shells, splinters and unburied bodies lie scattered far and wide." See: Norman Davies, *Rising '44: The Battle for Warsaw* (London: Macmillan, 2003), 404.

"The Four Horsemen" is dedicated to Barbara Szacka.

INVESTIGATION TWO / ICE

"The Final Era of Brightness"
While this section depicts, in part, the *"Illegal Age"* of the post-war period, it is not limited to one geographic location or period. Some details, however, refer to classic GULAG writings and other texts, such as *A Voice From the Chorus* and *One Day in the Life of Ivan Denisovich*.

The section Ice is dedicated to Robert Chandler.

(vi) *"...before the night extinguishes it..."* from Ewa Lipska, *White Strawberries* (Krakow: Wydawnictwo Literackie, 2000: Norton), 59.

(vii) *"...Your legs rattle like blue ice..."* from *Autumn Sonata, Selected Poems of Georg Trakl*, translated by Daniel Simko (Rhode Island: Asphodel Press, 1989), 127.

"The North"
"The North" is dedicated to Tomas Venclova.

(viii) *"...The prison always remains the center..."* from Abram Tertz (Andrei Sinyavsky) *A Voice from the Chorus* (New Haven: Yale University Press, 1995), 270.

(ix) *"...Green, yes, hung, yes, under spiteful skies..."* from *Selected Poems of Paul Celan* (New York: Norton, 2001), 125.

"The Denunciation"
"The Denunciation" is dedicated to Marie Luise Knott.

(x) *"...The black and white era which does not want to end..."* Aleksander Wat, in Czeslaw Milosz, *Postwar Polish Poetry* (Berkeley: University of California Press, 1985), 18.

"Rapid Debriefing"
"Rapid Debriefing" is dedicated to Lyudmila Alexeyeva, Moscow, 2012.

INVESTIGATION THREE / OBSCURITY

This section reflects on the advent of a new, and yet uncharted, "Illegal Age."

(xi) "...*Word, be that part of us, enlightened, clear and beautiful...*" from *The Collected Poems of Ingeborg Bachmann* (New York: Marsilio publishers, 1994), 181.

(xii) "...*For night unfolds the map, keeps secret its aim...*" from *The Collected Poems of Ingeborg Bachmann* (New York: Marsilio publishers, 1994), 119.

"On the Principles of the New Logic"
"On the Principles of the New Logic" is dedicated to John Friedman.

"The Illegal Age"
"The Illegal Age" is dedicated to Nora Krall.

(xiii) "...*The unspeakable... steals over the land...*" from *In the Storm of Roses: Selected Poems of Ingeborg Bachmann* (Princeton: Princeton University Press, 1986), 51.

(xiv) "...*Tell me, love, what I cannot explain...*" from *The Collected Poems of Ingeborg Bachmann* (Brookline: Zephyr Press, 2006), 163.

(xv) "...*Our godhead, History, has reserved us a grave...*" from *The Collected Poems of Ingeborg Bachmann* (Brookline: Zephyr Press, 2006), 55.

"Justice"
"Justice" is dedicated to S. Kandaouroff.

The Illegal Age explores the continuity and variations of the autocratic experience. Its three sections follow a R/E/F - I/R -E/F/T pattern, alternating lyrics, aphorisms, anti-lyrics and internal reports.

BIOGRAPHICAL NOTE

ELLEN HINSEY has published eight books of poetry, essays, dialogue and literary translation. Her most recent book is *Mastering the Past: Contemporary Central and Eastern Europe and the Rise of Illiberalism* (essays, Telos Press, 2017). Her other volumes of poetry include *Cities of Memory*, which received the Yale Series Award, *The White Fire of Time* and *Update on the Descent*, a National Poetry Series Finalist, which draws on her experience at the International Criminal Tribunal for the Former Yugoslavia in The Hague. *Magnetic North: Conversations with Tomas Venclova / Ellen Hinsey* explores ethical experience under totalitarianism.

A former faculty member of Skidmore College's Paris programme, she has been the recipient of numerous awards, including Lannan and Rona Jaffe Foundation fellowships. Hinsey's work has appeared in publications such as *Poetry Review*, *The New York Times*, *The New Yorker*, *The Irish Times*, *The Paris Review* and *Poetry*, and selections have appeared in French, Italian, German, Danish, Polish, Lithuanian, Serbian, and Arabic translation.

She lives in Paris and is the International Correspondent for *The New England Review*.